W9-AUI-091

Effective Parenting
in a Defective World

Chip Ingram

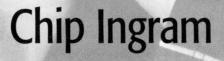

WALK
THRU THE
BIBLE

How to use this workbook.

Effective Parenting in a Defective World is designed to revolutionize your view of parenting. In nine sessions, you will discover powerful principles that will free you up to be an effective parent despite your surroundings. Each one of the nine video lessons is accompanied by probing discussion questions, exercises, and assignments to do at home. Whether you start the process alone or as part of a group, we strongly encourage you to view just one of the video sessions per week to allow the points of each message to sink in.

Video Course Notes.

In each session section, you'll find fill-in-the-blank questions that follow along with the video point by point. As you watch the video, write down key points and Scriptures. This is a vital part of the learning process, a way to make sure you retain what you learn.

Small Group Discussion Questions.

Following the video course notes for each session, you will find a set of compelling questions to use for group discussion. These questions are designed to uncover the heart of each individual, and to expose your pre-existing beliefs. As you discuss your answers together in the group, you will quicken the process of transformation as you affirm and encourage each other.

Action Steps.

Your group discussion time includes Action Steps, which are designed to help you move toward specific ways to apply the material. Your time will be enriched as you brainstorm new ideas with each other around the group.

At Home.

These in-depth, personal studies are intended to take the principles right off the page and into your personal life. This is where the series moves from contemplation to application. As you immerse yourself in these materials each day, the transformation process begins. It is important that you complete these assignments weekly.

Contents

*Can you really be an effective parent
in this defective world?*

CHIP INGRAM

PRESIDENT OF WALK THRU THE BIBLE® AND TEACHING PASTOR OF LIVING ON THE EDGE®

In my heart of hearts, that's the question I'm longing to answer for you. Because the answer is a resounding Yes! If you don't take anything else away from this series, I hope you'll remember that God is big enough to make you an effective parent no matter what the circumstances.

In fact, that's His goal.

How do I know? Because I've been there; I'm still there. I'm not just teaching about parenting theory. I'm also living it out, because I'm a parent just like you. I've made some big mistakes. But I'm here to tell you that being an effective parent doesn't mean always being a "perfect" parent. In the coming weeks together, I look forward to sharing how God has shown up in my parenting despite my shortcomings. And He longs to do the same for you.

From Joseph to David to Mary, God has been using young people to show His almighty power for thousands of years. He's big enough to draw your child to Himself as well. The question is how can we, as parents, help that process? I'll give you a hint: you don't have to be an expert in child psychology or have a doctorate in Bible theology; all you need is a willing heart and some basic principles. Then you can watch as God moves in to make you an effective parent despite the world around you.

That means you don't have to keep your kids in a plastic bubble. And you don't have to fear what the world throws at you. We live in a time of unprecedented challenges for parents. However, the good news is that when there is darkness, God's light of truth appears even brighter. I look forward to these next few weeks together when we will discover how God can take your desire for His will and use it to make you an effective parent in a defective world.

Chip Ingram
President, Walk Thru the Bible®
and Teaching Pastor of Living On The Edge®

How to Raise Positive Kids in a Negative World

*T*mes have changed. Just a few generations ago, getting in trouble meant talking too much in class or being disrespectful to your elders. But today, the stakes are much higher. The common entry-level offenses for school-age kids today often include drinking, experimenting with drugs, sexual activity, and recreational crime. One small slip-up and a young person can find his life permanently altered, or ended altogether. It's a very negative world.

God isn't taken by surprise. In fact, He's been using teenagers to change their world for thousands of years. And He can still equip you to be an effective parent in your world. First, you need a picture of what He's trying to accomplish through your parenting. In this session, we'll reveal the power of parenting with vision as we uncover the keys to raising positive kids in a negative world.

How to Raise Positive Kids in a Negative World

Principles for Positive Parenting

1. Positive parenting begins with ——————————— ,

clear-cut ———————————— .

Fathers, don't overcorrect your children or make it difficult for them to obey the commandment. Bring them up with Christian teaching in Christian discipline. Ephesians 6:4 (Phillips)

The Principle of ————————— .

God's dream vs. the world's dream for your child.

. . . to be conformed to the likeness of his Son. Romans 8:29b

2. Positive parenting demands we _____ what we _____ .

More is caught than taught

14 I am not writing this to shame you, but to warn you, as my dear children. 15 Even though you have ten thousand guardians in Christ, you do not have many fathers, for in Christ Jesus I became your father through the gospel. 16 Therefore I urge you to imitate me. 1 Corinthians 4:14–16

The Principle of _____ .

A student is not above his teacher, but everyone who is fully trained will be like his teacher. Luke 6:40

Questions

1 If you had to name one area in your life where you are not modeling the kind of person you want your child to become, what would it be? In other words, what is it about you that needs to change to become what you want your child to model?

2 The media highlights shootings, drug use, and drunk driving as some of the defects young people face growing up today. Everybody has different concerns. What are the top five issues/defects that concern you when you consider the threats facing your child and your parenting?
List them below:

3 What are some ways you parent with focus; that is, out of your positive objectives?
Give examples.

4 What are some ways you parent out of fear? Give examples.

5 Which type of parent are you most of the time—one who parents with focus, or one who parents out of fear?

In the space
below, describe your personal target for successful parenting. However you
define success, describe it now. Share your answers with the group.

Examples: "I want to teach my child one new character trait every month (such as obedience), including memorizing a definition and acting out scenarios where the character trait is important in life," or "I will take Johnny to the Father/Son retreat every year," or "Sarah will take care of her own laundry by age 12 and prepare one meal a month for our family starting at age 15," etc.

List of "WHATS"

Now try to give a "why" for each item you listed above. Again, share
your answers with the group.

Examples: If you said, "I will teach Bobby how to divide his allowance, giving a tenth to the church, saving a tenth for the future, and carefully stewarding the rest toward wise purchases;" for this exercise you might say, "My purpose is to teach Bobby how to be a good steward and to understand that everything belongs to God and is simply managed by us."

List of "WHYS"

Application

This week, casually observe your parenting patterns as you interact with your child.

Next week, be prepared to discuss the following with the group:

1 What are some positive ways your child models the examples you have lived out in front of him or her?

_____

_____

_____

_____

2 What are some negative ways your child models your example?

_____

_____

_____

3 Write down and report back to your group at least one step you took this week to change the way you model for your child.

_____

_____

_____

_____

4 Spend some time studying 1 Corinthians 4:14-16. Read it several times, along with any study notes you might have available. Be prepared to share one insight from this passage with your group to encourage them to be positive parents.

_____

_____

_____

_____

Building Relationships that Bond

*P*arenting brings with it the certainty that there will be times when the going gets rough. There will be conflict that threatens the love between parent and child. It's not a matter of *if*, but *when*. The good news is that being an effective parent doesn't mean knowing how to avoid those times, it simply means knowing how to navigate through them. God's plan is not to circumvent the storms, but to build a foundation strong enough to weather them.

There is a tendency to think that conflict is an indication of weakness in a relationship, but nothing could be further from the truth. Conflict is simply a by-product of the defective world in which we live. The strength of a relationship is measured by how well it endures conflict. Strong relationships don't just happen; they must be cultivated in a certain type of family environment. In this session, we will learn *8 Keys for Building Relationships That Bond*.

Relationships

Building Relationships that Bond

A Biblical Picture of Parenting
(Continued from Session 1)

 3. Positive parents build relationships that _____.

A Picture of How God Parents

Like a mother:

⁷…but we were gentle among you, like a mother caring for her little children. ⁸We loved you so much that we were delighted to share with you not only the gospel of God but our lives as well, because you had become so dear to us.
1 Thessalonians 2:7–8

Like a father:

¹¹For you know that we dealt with each of you as a father deals with his own children, ¹²encouraging, comforting and urging you to live lives worthy of God, who calls you into his kingdom and glory.
1 Thessalonians 2:11–12

The Principle of _____.

Axiom 1: The _____ your relationship with your child, the _____ likely he will embrace your values and beliefs.

Axiom 2: The _____ your relationship with your child, the _____ likely he will embrace your values and beliefs.

Axiom 3: Tension and stress and difficulties are _____.

Parent's Lifestyle	Strength of Relationship	Child's Lifestyle
Values + Beliefs		Values + Beliefs

8 Keys for Building Relationships that Bond:

1 _____ Love

2 _____ Time

3 Focused _____

4 _____ Contact

5 _____ Communication

6 Meaningful _____

- Dinner _____

7 Have _____ Together

- _____

8 _____ Together Often

- Shared _____

4. Positive parenting requires constant _____ and ongoing _____ .

When you blow it:

If we confess our sins, he is faithful and just and will forgive us our sins and purify us from all unrighteousness. 1 John 1:9

The Principle of _____ .

Five Powerful Words: _____ _____ . _____ _____ .

1   Of the *8 Keys for Building Relationships that Bond*, which one or two areas need the most repair? Share your answers with the group.

2   Of the *8 Keys for Building Relationships that Bond*, which two are you the best at doing? Share your answers with the group.

3   After you share your answer from #2 above, pick one area to work on and ask your group for suggestions to improve in that area. In the space below, indicate which one you will work on and write their suggestions:

4   On a scale of 1 to 10, how strong is the bond between you and your child?

What's one way the group can pray for you as you seek to build a strong relationship bond with your child this week? Discuss.

Review your findings from last week with the group: What are some positive ways your child models the examples you have lived out in front of him or her?

What are some negative ways your child models your example?

Report back to your group at least one step you took this week to change the way you model for your child.

Spend some time studying 1 Corinthians 4:14-16.
Read it several times, along with any study notes you might have available. Be prepared to share some insights with your group on how this passage has encouraged you to be a positive parent.

Application

This week, schedule time alone with your child or children. Where age-appropriate, briefly describe each of the *8 Keys for Building Relationships that Bond* to your child. Ask your child to pick one or two that are most appealing. Then ask him or her to pick the least appealing. Finally, ask your child if he or she has any additional suggestions that weren't on the list. Be prepared to share your findings with the group next week.

1   Most appealing:

2   Least appealing:

3   Additional suggestions:

Potential 3

How to Develop Your Child's Full Potential

*H*ow do you define success in parenting. Is it raising an academically superior child? Is it raising a child who excels in athletics? Or maybe just producing a well-rounded kid? Just to be on the safe side, many parents adopt the strategy of giving their child every available opportunity, helping him advance in sports, academics, and social arenas. Depending on where you live, your culture may emphasize status, financial accomplishments, or your profession. To complicate matters further, different families have preferences of their own that they emphasize.

What does God think? Despite the varieties of opinions around the world, God offers a very clear definition of success. And it may surprise you. If you want to know how to develop your child's full potential, you must first understand how God defines success. In this session, you will learn the single most important factor that determines success or failure for your child. Until you do, your child can never reach his full potential.

3

How to Develop Your Child's Full Potential

Potential

God Has a Dream

1. You must understand your child's two primary needs are

for _____ and _____.

Two questions kids are always asking:

Do you _____ me?

Where are the _____ ?

The Perfect Parent:

So God created man in his own image, in the image of God he created him; male and female he created them. Genesis 1:27

[15]The LORD God took the man and put him in the Garden of Eden to work it and take care of it. [16]And the LORD God commanded the man, "You are free to eat from any tree in the garden; [17]but you must not eat from the tree of the knowledge of good and evil, for when you eat of it you will surely die." Genesis 2:15-17

 2. You must recognize your child's primary responsibility

is to learn _____ .

[1]Children, it is your Christian duty to obey your parents, for this is the right thing to do. [2]"Respect your father and mother" is the first commandment that has a promise added: [3]so that all may go well with you, and you may live a long time in the land. Ephesians 6:1-3 (Good News Bible)

Defining Obedience:

Obedience is teaching your child to come under the hearing of your voice.

[21]Whoever has my commands and obeys them, he is the one who loves me. He who loves me will be loved by my Father, and I too will love him and show myself to him. John 14:21

3. Obedience is a _____ _____ .

Although he was a son, he learned obedience from what he suffered…
Hebrews 5:8

And Jesus grew in wisdom and stature, and in favor with God and men.
Luke 2:52

Wisdom = _____   Stature = _____

Favor with God = _____

Favor with men = _____

SPIRITUAL FORMATION AND MENTAL DEVELOPMENT				
	Rules	**Relationship**	**Reasons**	**Resolve**
AGE:	0 – 4 or 5	6 – 7	11 – 12	16 – 17
Concrete Thinking ⟶				Adult Abstract Thinking

Knowledge axiom:

_____ + _____ + _____ = _____

1. **Principle of** _____ – Only teach children what they are mentally and emotionally capable of learning.

2. **Principle of** _____ – Never routinely do for your children what they can do for themselves.

Parents, do not treat your children in such a way as to make them angry. Instead, raise them with Christian discipline and instruction.
Ephesians 6:4 (Good News Bible)

Questions

1 What are the top one or two behavioral issues you have with your child? Share your answers with the group.

2 On a scale of 1 to 10, how would you rate your adherence to the Principle of Readiness in your parenting? Share at least one specific example with the group.

3 On a scale of 1 to 10, how would you rate your adherence to the Principle of Responsibility in your parenting? Share at least one specific example with the group.

4 Do you tend to talk too much or too little in your parenting? Why is this helpful or harmful?

Now that you've identified your top one or two behavioral issues,

what will it look like for you to begin changing your parenting to improve how you help your child reach his full potential? It might be teaching your child that you mean what you say. It could be explaining your decisions to your toddler less often, or explaining them more to your teenager. Write your answer in the space below, then share it with the group.

What is one step you could take this week to begin changing

this aspect of your parenting? Share your idea with the group and ask for their feedback.

Review your findings from last week with the group:

Last week, you spent scheduled time alone with your child or children, and described the *8 Keys for Building Relationships that Bond.* Which two did he or she say were most appealing? Least appealing? Were there any additional suggestions that weren't on the list?

Most Appealing	Least Appealing	Additional Suggestions

Application

One of the most important responsibilities you have as a parent is to be a good student of your children. Do you truly understand your child's unique need for significance? For security?

1 **This week, ask your child** what kinds of things make him or her feel special and loved. It may take some time and conversing to get your child to open up. Perhaps you can ask your child what one or two things you already do that make him or her feel loved. Or what things your child wishes you would start doing, or do more. Describe your findings in the space below. Be prepared to share them with the group.

2 **Next, ask your child** what kinds of things make him or her feel secure. Your child may not give the "right" answer such as, "When you enforce the boundaries." But just listen and observe anyway. Try to notice any sensitivities, fears, concerns, or other issues you haven't seen before. Avoid correcting your child. Just listen. If he or she introduces a concern, follow it. Probe a little. Get to know the side of your child that craves security. Describe your findings in the space below. Be prepared to share them with the group.

God's Process for Teaching Obedience

O bedience is something every parent strives for. As we've seen, it's the one thing God commands of our children. Whether your goal is to develop the holiness of your child, or simply bring order to your household, obedience is an attractive concept. There's just one question. How do you do it? Just because you desire obedience from your child doesn't mean he wants it. So what do you do? Where do you start?

We've already learned that developing obedience is a process, not an event. Moreover, it's a process designed by God and mandated for your child. Whenever God calls you to a goal, He always provides the resources to reach it. In this session, we'll explore five resources that will help you stay in the developmental process of obedience in your parenting. Along the way, we'll discover what complete obedience looks like when you've reached the finish line.

4

God's Process for Teaching Obedience

How to Develop Your Child's Full Potential (Continued from Session 3)

 4. You must commit to providing the necessary

_____ for your child to learn _____.

⁴Hear, O Israel! The LORD is our God, the LORD is one! ⁵And you shall love the LORD your God with all your heart and with all your soul and with all your might. ⁶And these words, which I am commanding you today, shall be on your heart; ⁷and you shall teach them diligently to your sons and shall talk of them when you sit in your house and when you walk by the way and when you lie down and when you rise up. ⁸And you shall bind them as a sign on your hand and they shall be as frontals on your forehead. ⁹And you shall write them on the doorposts of your house and on your gates. Deuteronomy 6:4-9 (NAS)

5 RESOURCES YOUR CHILDREN NEED FROM YOU:

FIVE Teachable

FOUR Systematic

THREE Biblical

TWO Personal

ONE Doctrinal

How do you know when you have hit the target?

Obedience is achieved when your child has —————————

his or her primary love, submission and dependency from

————————— to ————————— ————————— .

Three Characteristics of Righteous Children:

1. They make wise ————————— .

[9]And this is my prayer: that your love may abound more and more in knowledge and depth of insight, [10]so that you may be able to discern what is best and may be pure and blameless until the day of Christ, [11]filled with the fruit of righteousness that comes through Jesus Christ — to the glory and praise of God.
Philippians 1:9–11

2. They keep their ————————— .

Many a man claims to have unfailing love, but a faithful man who can find?
Proverbs 20:6

3. They care genuinely for ————————— .

Greater love has no one than this, that he lay down his life for his friends.
John 15:13

Questions

1 Of the Five Resources discussed in this session, which one comes most naturally for you as a parent? Share your answer with the group.

2 Which one needs the most work? Is there a particular area that seems to be a common challenge to the parents in your group?

3 God's Word says that obedience is your child's greatest responsibility. In contrast to this, what are some of the things the culture around you says about children and their responsibilities?

4 What does it mean to say that obedience is the channel for God's blessing?

Which of the Five Resources discussed in this session does your child need the most from you?

5 RESOURCES
YOUR CHILDREN
NEED FROM
YOU:

FIVE	Teachable
FOUR	Systematic
THREE	Biblical
TWO	Personal
ONE	Doctrinal

Describe one step you can take today to begin building that resource into your daily life. Put it into practice today. Be prepared to share the results with the group.

Review your findings from last week with the group:

Last week, you became a student of your child's heart. You discussed with your child what makes him feel loved and what makes him feel secure. Share your findings with the group.

Application

This week, write a letter to your child that will be opened on his or her 21st birthday. In this brief letter, share your thoughts and ambitions about obedience. Describe your hopes and dreams. Explain your heartaches and frustrations. Pour your heart out. Articulate why obedience is important to you. Be honest about your failures and shortcomings. Express your greatest desires for your child's journey toward a life of obedience.

Dear _____ /_____

_____

_____

_____

_____

_____

_____

_____

_____

_____

_____

_____

_____

_____

_____

_____

_____

_____

_____

How to Discipline Your Child Effectively

We've just learned five resources for cultivating obedience in your child. Those resources provide the indispensable foundation for your child to begin growing through the developmental process of obedience. Now it's time to get practical. In this session, we will tackle the question: How should you discipline your child?

In many ways, this is the chapter you've been waiting for. It may be the reason you sought parenting instruction in the first place. Everybody wants to know what to do when their child won't obey. In this session, we'll discover just that. In addition, we'll uncover four classic parenting styles that will help you understand what kind of parent you really are. And we'll describe a parenting style from God's Word that every parent will want to emulate.

How to Discipline Your Child Effectively

Discipline

Two Case Studies

Case Study #1: The Reuben Hill Minnesota Report

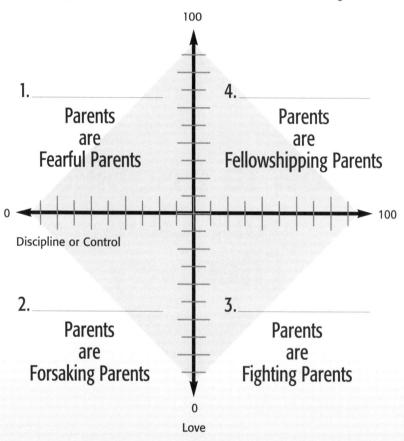

1. Parents are Fearful Parents

4. Parents are Fellowshipping Parents

2. Parents are Forsaking Parents

3. Parents are Fighting Parents

Discipline or Control

Love

100

0

100

0

Summary– The balanced, authoritative parent who combines high levels of support with high levels of control typically produced children with high self-esteem, good coping skills, and a positive relationship with parents.

Case Study #2: Hebrews 12 – Christians AD 66-70

[4]In your struggle against sin, you have not yet resisted to the point of shedding your blood. [5]And you have forgotten that word of encouragement that addresses you as sons:

> *"My son, do not make light of the Lord's discipline, and do not lose heart when he rebukes you, [6]because the Lord disciplines those he loves, and he punishes * everyone he accepts as a son."*

[7]Endure hardship as discipline; God is treating you as sons. For what son is not disciplined by his father? [8]If you are not disciplined (and everyone undergoes discipline), then you are illegitimate children and not true sons. [9]Moreover, we have all had human fathers who disciplined us and we respected them for it. How much more should we submit to the Father of our spirits and live! [10]Our fathers disciplined us for a little while as they thought best; but God disciplines us for our good, that we may share in his holiness. [11]No discipline seems pleasant at the time, but painful. Later on, however, it produces a harvest of righteousness and peace for those who have been trained by it. Hebrews 12:4-11

* A better translation of "punishes" is "chastens" or "educates."

Summary – Discipline is teaching obedience to God and His Word through consistent consequences (actions) and clear instructions (words) in an atmosphere of love.

[11]My son, do not despise the LORD'S discipline and do not resent his rebuke, [12]because the LORD disciplines those he loves, as a father the son he delights in. Proverbs 3:11-12

Five Characteristics of Discipline:

1. **The necessity of discipline –** To deter _____ *(verse 4)*

2. **The means of discipline –** The _____ and _____ *(verse 5)*

3. **The motive in discipline –** To express _____ *(verses 6-9)*

4. **The goal of discipline –** To teach _____ *(verse 9)*

5. **The result of discipline –** Short-term _____ and

   long-term _____ *(verses 10-11)*

Questions

1   Which of the four parenting styles best describes you? _____

2   Which one best describes the way you were parented? _____

3   How does the way you were parented impact this area of your parenting?

4   In your own words, what is the greatest benefit of discipline?

From your discussion of the four parenting styles, would you say you need to be more firm, or more loving? Why?

What are some specific ways you can begin to be more firm or more loving in your home this week? Perhaps you need to have a conversation with your child about this week's lesson and the changes you plan to make. Discuss your ideas with the group and ask for suggestions. Write an action plan in the space below.

Action Plan:

Review your findings from last week with the group:

Last week, you wrote a letter to your child in which you shared your heart's desire for his or her obedience. You may share your letter with the group. If you prefer, you may simply summarize some of the insights you discovered in the process of writing the letter.

Application

This week try to catch yourself exhibiting one of the four parenting styles. It can be a desirable example or one that's not so desirable, but it needs to be a real-life experience from this week. Describe the scenario briefly below. Be prepared to share your example with the group.

Punishment Versus Discipline

S panking can be a controversial topic. But most of the controversy stems from how it has been misused. Unfortunately, the mention of spanking conjures images of oppression and abuse with some people. But that's not how chastisement is portrayed in the Bible. Through an honest, open-minded examination of Scripture, we can begin to see an accurate picture of biblical concepts like spanking.

At the heart of biblical spanking is the notion that its purpose is one of love. Parenting can have its moments of frustration, but that should never be a motivation for discipline. Biblical spanking is to be a selfless act that guides the child toward wisdom. In this session, we'll see how God's attitude toward us is a model for the parent's attitude toward the child during discipline.

6

Discipline

Punishment Versus Discipline

Knowing the Difference Between Punishment and Discipline–

	PUNISHMENT	DISCIPLINE
Purpose	To inflict penalty for an offense	To train for correction and maturity
Focus	Past Misdeeds	Future correct acts
Attitude	Hostility and frustration on the part of the parent	Love and concern on the part of the parent
Resulting Emotion in the Child	Fear and guilt	Security

Two Key Biblical Concepts:

1. Actions = Consistent

The Biblical Concept of Spanking –

He who spares his rod hates his son, but he who loves him disciplines him diligently. Proverbs 13:24 (NAS)

Folly is bound up in the heart of a child, but the rod of discipline will drive it far from him. Proverbs 22:15

Seven Steps to Discipline:

1. Clear _____

2. Establish _____

3. Avoid _____

4. Communicate _____

5. Flick the _____

6. Sincere _____

7. Unconditional _____

1 What is your reaction to the words in Proverbs 13:24 and Proverbs 22:15? Do the words in Proverbs seem blunt? Do you agree with them completely? Explain.

2 How has your own upbringing impacted your views on spanking?

3 List several words to describe the attitude of someone giving a punishment:

4 List several words to describe the attitude of someone practicing discipline:

In the space below, list several examples of situations in which you intend to use spanking.

Examples: "When my child deliberately defies me," "When Jeffrey talks back disrespectfully and intentionally," "Only when I have given clear warning first."

Scenarios	Situations	Stipulations

In contrast, what are some examples of situations in which you would use other forms of correction?

Examples: "For minor infractions," "When Jeffrey forgets to answer properly, I will correct him verbally instead";"When another consequence is more logical (such as taking away a privilege to correct misuse of that privilege)."

Scenarios	Situations	Stipulations

For you personally, which of the following is most likely to prevent you from modeling biblical spanking in your parenting:

___ Lack of belief in spanking   ___ Too soft-hearted to inflict pain on my child

___ Unable to manage frustration/anger and portray love/gentleness while spanking

___ Too difficult to spank consistently

Review your findings from last week with the group:

Last week you observed your parenting, looking for examples of the four parenting styles. Share one or two real-life examples with the group—whether desirable or not so desirable.

Application

There are many forces that shape our parenting philosophies—whether positively or negatively. In fact, they are so prevalent that most of the time we don't give them much thought. But their subtle messages can pressure us to believe one way or another. Among these forces are the media, the opinions of family/friends, and your own life experience. This week, try to notice at least one factor that influences your view of spanking. Describe the situation, the influencing factor, and what its message says about spanking. Share your example with the group.

Words That Discipline

*T*here's no doubt about it—biblical parenting sometimes requires taking decisive action. But it also requires decisive speech. The Bible speaks of the power of "a word fitly spoken." In fact, sometimes words can do what actions can't. Clearly, the combination of actions and words are God's recipe for the discipleship of parenting.

In this session, we delve into discipline's other half—words. Hidden in the original Hebrew are important clues to help us uncover the meaning of the Bible's instructions for using words as a tool to bring about correction in parenting. We also look at four ways to use words properly, as well as common pitfalls to avoid.

Words That Discipline

Correction

Two Key Biblical Concepts (Continued)

2. Words = Clear _____

_____

_____

[11]My son, do not reject the discipline of the LORD, Or loathe His reproof, [12]For whom the LORD loves He reproves, Even as a father, the son in whom he delights. Proverbs 3:11-12 (NAS)

Four Ways To Use Words To Bring About Correction:

1. Say "_____" Firmly.

_____

2. _____ age-appropriately.

_____

3. Use _____.

_____

4. Use _____.

_____

_____

_____

Practical Tips for Balanced Parenting

Avoid these Pitfalls:

- _____ Parent

- _____ – _____ Parent

- _____ Parent

- _____ – _____ Parent

- _____ – _____ Parent

Develop a Game Plan:

- Identify the top two _____ problems.

- Honestly evaluate your present parenting _____.

- Have a family _____.

- Join hands together and _____.

1 Which, if any, of the pitfalls discussed describes you? Honestly identify any areas you need to improve and list them below. Then share your answers with the group. Remember, it may not be possible to be perfect, but at least you can be honest.

2 What are the top two behavior problems you face right now with your children? Share your situation with the group.

3 How might your parenting have contributed to each of these problems?

4 What would it take to begin resolving those issues? Develop a first step in your game plan and share it with the group. Ask for their feedback and suggestions.

5 Why is it important to say "no" firmly?

An important part of discipline is teaching your child to own the

consequences of his or her actions. One way to do this is with contracts. When your child clearly understands the consequences that will result from inappropriate behavior, you transfer full responsibility for the outcome to him or her. Identify one way you can use a contract to transfer responsibility to your child. Describe the situation in the space below. Also include how you plan to agree on a suitable consequence with your child. Share your plan with the group.

Transfer of Responsibility:	Suitable Consequence:

Review your findings from last week with the group:

Last week, you were to notice at least one factor that influences your view of spanking. Share your example with the group, including the situation, the influencing factor, and what its message said about spanking.

Application

This week, hold a family conference to discuss your top behavior concerns. Be open, honest, and transparent. Avoid the instinct to be "right" in front of your child. Allow him or her to see that you are working on being a godly parent. Ask your child to share his or her perceptions on the subject. Be firm about your God-given responsibilities to provide a balance of love and boundaries in your parenting. Invite suggestions for what works and what doesn't. Pray together as a family, asking God to help each of you become what He wants you to be. Be prepared to share a brief report about the experience with your group.

(To your child) How am I a good parent?

(To your child) How can I improve?

(To your child) One thing you can do that would help me be a better parent is . . .

Five Smooth Stones for Parenting

W hen it comes to parenting, there are a lot of tips and principles to remember. Already, we've covered a significant amount of material. By the time you complete this series, you could feel a little overwhelmed by the volume of information. And in the heat of battle, it can be challenging to keep it all straight. That's why you need a few, simple anchor points to cling to. So in this session, we'll begin our look at five basic tenets that will prepare your child to win life's biggest battles. If you focus on these, everything else will fall into place.

Parenting is a tough job. But so is being a child growing up in the world today. There are many giants to face. And unless your child has the right ammunition, he can end up a victim of fear, temptation, or compromise. God has been in the business of equipping children for life's battles for thousands of years. And He can help you equip yours for the battles of his or her lifetime.

8

Principles

Five Smooth Stones for Parenting

How to Prepare Your Kids to Win Life's Biggest Battles

Stone #1: Teach Them to _____ Well.

A Theology of Suffering:

- Life is hard, but God is _____ !

- Life is unjust, but God is _____ .

- Old Testament Roots (Joseph) — Genesis 37-50

- New Testament Command – 1 Peter 2:21-23

21 To this you were called, because Christ suffered for you, leaving you an example, that you should follow in his steps. 22 "He committed no sin, and no deceit was found in his mouth." 23 When they hurled their insults at him, he did not retaliate; when he suffered, he made no threats. Instead, he entrusted himself to him who judges justly. 1 Peter 2:21-23

Application: Help your child grow through suffering.

How to teach your kids to grow through suffering:

1. Find out what they're _____ about

   and _____ about it.

2. Find out _____ they're suffering.

3. Align _____ with their suffering.

Life Message: Suffering is _____ .

Stone #2: Teach Them to _____ "Unto the Lord."

A Theology of Work:

- Work is a "_____", not a job.

- All work is _____ .

- Our work is to flow from God's unique design and

  _____ for our lives.

- Work is for "an audience of _____."

- Old Testament Roots — Genesis 2:15

- New Testament Command — Colossians 3:23

Application: Help your child discover God's _____ for his life so he can impact their world and beyond.

How to teach your kids to work unto the Lord:

1. Weekly _____ that they do with a good attitude.

2. Study their_____ .

_____

_____

Life Message: You were _____ to work.

_____

_____

8

Principles

Five Smooth Stones for Parenting

Stone #3: Teach Them to _____ Their Lives Wisely.

A Theology of Stewardship:

- God owns _____ .

- God has entrusted things – time, talent, and

  _____ – to us to manage for Him.

- God expects a _____ return on His investment.

- God will hold you _____ .

- God wants you to share in His _____ .

- Old Testament Roots — Genesis 1:26-28

- New Testament Command — Matthew 25:14-30

Application: Help your child become _____ **in the little things. (Luke 16:10)**

How to teach your kids to be faithful in the little things:

1. Teach your children the three purposes of money:

   _____ , saving, and spending.

2. Teach your children to _____ ahead.

Life Message: Your life is a _____ stewardship.

Questions

1 Is it possible to avoid suffering in this day and age? Discuss.

2 In the name of keeping a "positive mental attitude," many parents ignore suffering, sweeping it under the rug. How can you prepare your child for times of suffering without creating a negative outlook? Share your ideas with the group.

3 What do you think is the greatest cause of concern – the greatest source of suffering – for your child today?

4 What are some ways you could interact with your child to teach him or her how to suffer well? Share your ideas with the group.

5 On a scale of 1-10, how would you rate your child's work ethic? Give examples.

In the space below, list several words that describe your work ethic:

Does having a strong work ethic mean the same thing as working "unto the Lord?" Explain.

Review your findings from last week with the group:

Last week, you held a family conference to discuss the top two behavior problems you face right now with your children. Briefly share the results of that meeting with the group.

Application

This week, you will take definitive steps to become a student of your child by asking a few probing questions to get to know his or her heart. You may record your answers below. Be prepared to share your answers with the group.

1 (To your child) "What are you most concerned about?"

2 (To your child) "What makes you feel afraid?"

3 Now you'll take steps to become a student of your child's vocational calling in life. In the space below, describe your child's favorite things, his or her dreams and what he or she excels at the most? Try to make observations that could be clues to your child's God-given calling. Be prepared to share your findings with the group.

My child's favorite things:

My child's dreams:

What my child excels at the most:

9

Principles

When All Else Fails

*I*n this final session, we take on two observations that may be the most important nuggets in parenting. First, in the coming years, there will be a handful of decisions your child will make that will change the course of his or her life forever. The most important thing you can do is equip him or her to make wise decisions. As we're about to see, your child's ability to choose wisely hinges on his ongoing pursuit of holiness.

The second observation is that your child will know the taste of failure. Failure is inevitable in every life, and rather than try to avoid it, the wise parent teaches his or her child how to leverage it for even greater success. The key to turning failure into success is a deep understanding of grace. Within the freedom and security of a grace-filled life, your child can face the most disappointing experiences and overcome them.

Principles

Five Smooth Stones for Parenting (Continued)

Stone #4: Teach Them to Make _____ Choices.

A Theology of Holiness:

- God is high, _____ , "totally other."

- God is absolute _____ .

- God's _____ defines absolute truth.

- God's _____ (morals) are for our protection.

- God's ultimate aim is to make us _____ .

- Old Testament Roots — Exodus 3:5-6

- New Testament Command — 1 Peter 1:15-16

Application: Help your child to _____ **between good and evil.**

How to teach your kids to make wise choices:

1. Start when they're _____ .

2. _____ to them.

3. Monitor their _____ to the media.

Life Message: Holy living allows you to experience

God's _____ for your life.

9

When All Else Fails

Principles

Stone #5: Teach Them to Live _____ – _____ Lives.

A Theology of Grace:

- Grace is the unmerited and unconditional _____ of God toward us.

- Grace is free to us, but _____ to God.

- The _____ is God's greatest act of grace.

- _____ is a free gift from God.

- Grace must be _____ by faith.

- Grace produces _____ toward God, and love toward others.

- Old Testament Roots—Genesis 3:21

- New Testament Command—Ephesians 2:8-10; 1 Peter 1:13

Application: Help your child realize that _____ **is never final with God.**

How to teach your kids that failure is never final:

1. Be a safe place for your child by asking, "How can I _____?"

2. Show your child how to _____.

Life Message: You were created to _____ grace and to give grace.

1 Read the following passage aloud:

For the reverence and fear of God are basic to all wisdom. Knowing God results in every other kind of understanding. Proverbs 9:10 (TLB)

What does this passage suggest about the role of holiness in obtaining wisdom?

_____

_____

2 Explain the statement: "God's law is for our protection."

_____

3 Read the following passage aloud:

[15]I don't understand myself at all, for I really want to do what is right, but I can't. I do what I don't want to—what I hate. [16]I know perfectly well that what I am doing is wrong, and my bad conscience proves that I agree with these laws I am breaking. [17]But I can't help myself, because I'm no longer doing it. It is sin inside me that is stronger than I am that makes me do these evil things.

[24,25]So you see how it is: my new life tells me to do right, but the old nature that is still inside me loves to sin. Oh, what a terrible predicament I'm in! Who will free me from my slavery to this deadly lower nature? Thank God! It has been done by Jesus Christ our Lord. He has set me free. Romans 7:15-17; 24-25 (TLB)

What does this passage suggest about the likelihood of failure during your child's lifetime?

_____

_____

4 What does it suggest about God's perspective on failure?

_____

_____

_____

In the space below, list several words or phrases to describe the ideal way to respond when your child fails. Share your suggestions with the group.

Which one of the words or phrases above do you need to work on the most to begin modeling it in your parenting?

Review your findings from last week with the group:
Last week, you took steps to become a student of your child. Share your findings with the group.

Application

Failure–whether your child's or yours–is never final with God.
Did this session cause any of your parenting failures to stand out in your mind? If so, briefly describe it in the space below. If not, keep thinking. Then, go to your child and recall the experience, explaining how you think you may have failed. Describe how you could have responded instead. Ask for forgiveness. Children long to believe that their parents are good. They will overlook almost any offense to support this vision. Therefore, they are amazingly resilient when it comes to healing old wounds with forgiveness. Use this conversation time with your child to model that failure is never final with God.

1 (To your child) "I think I may have blown it as a parent the time I:"

2 (To your child) "Would you please forgive me?"